FEARFULLY & Wonderfully MADE

WRITTEN BY
CHARLIE I. EJIM

ILLUSTRATED BY
JOANNA PASEK

FEARFULLY & WONDERFULLY MADE

Copyright © 2024 **Charlie Books**

All rights reserved. No part of this publication may be reproduced, distributed, or transmitted in any form or by any means, including photocopying, recording, or other electronic or mechanical methods, without the prior written permission of the publisher, except in the case of brief quotations embodied in critical reviews and certain other noncommercial uses permitted by copyright law. For permission requests, write to the publisher, addressed "Attention: Book Rights and Permission," at the address below.

Published in the United States of America

ISBN 978-1-962730-46-4 (HC)
ISBN 978-1-962730-01-3 (Ebook)

Charlie Books
222 West 6th Street
Suite 400, San Pedro, CA, 90731
www.stellarliterary.com

Ordering Information and Rights Permission:
Quantity sales. Special discounts might be available on quantity purchases by corporations, associations, and others. For details, contact the publisher at the address above.

For Book Rights Adaptation and other Rights Permission. Call us at toll-free 1-888-945-8513 or send us an email at admin@stellarliterary.com.

"But the word is very near you. It is in your mouth and in your heart so that you can do it."
Deuteronomy 30:14 (ESV)

Fearfully & Wonderfully Made by Charlie I. Ejim
Copyright 2023 by Charlie I. Ejim

Illustration and Cover Art by Joanna Pasek
Designed and Edited by Qamber Designs & Media W.L.L.

To my parents
Thank you for making sure I know that I am loved.

To my creator
Thanks for making me, fearfully & wonderfully.
I owe everything I am to YOU.

I sing.
I swing and swim.
I skip and dance.

I climb and jump.
I cry, laugh and clap.
I praise.

PRAISE?
Say something nice or applaud. Show approval.

Congratulate, Compliment, Celebrate, Cheer on! A pat on the back.

I praise my mom.
I praise my dad.

I praise my teachers.
I praise my friends.
I praise myself.

you?
Who is you?

The LORD who provides.
The LORD who heals.
The LORD our peace.
The LORD who makes us holy.
The LORD our shepherd.
The LORD our banner.
God Almighty, The Creator!

I praise YOU because I am...

NOT
I was
(in the past)

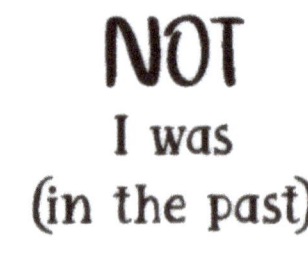

Or
I will be
(in the future).

I praise you because

I am fearfully...

fearfully!
With great affection and thoughtfulness.
With deep, genuine care.
With a whole lot of awe.

I praise you because
I am fearfully and...

Yes, there is more to you.

I praise you because
I am fearfully and wonderfully...

Yes,
 Unrivaled,
  Uniquely,
   One-of-a-kind,
    Extremely well.

I praise you because
I am fearfully and wonderfully

MADE!

MADE.
Formed.
Shaped.
Molded.
Crafted.
Created.

Yes, I am fearfully and wonderfully **MADE!**

Simply put, I AM A MASTERPIECE!

I praise you because I am fearfully and wonderfully made.
Psalm 139:14a

This is a fact!
AND, I know this fully well!

About the Author

Charlie I. Ejim is an educator and author. Amongst her many interests, she is passionate about teaching scriptures to the younger generation and making the Word more relatable to them. She currently lives in the Middle East with her husband, two teenage children and their Maltese terrier.

www.ingramcontent.com/pod-product-compliance
Lightning Source LLC
Chambersburg PA
CBHW061353010526
44107CB00011B/922